ONE HUNDRED WAYS TO

*A Beautiful
Garden*

ONE HUNDRED WAYS TO

*A Beautiful
Garden*

BY

Jane Owen

Illustrations by

Jilly Wilkinson

HODDER &
STOUGHTON

Text Copyright © 2006 by Jane Owen
Illustrations Copyright © 2006 by Jilly Wilkinson

First published in Great Britain in 2006

British Library Cataloguing in Publication Data
A record for this book is available from the British Library

ISBN – 10: 0 340 91008 9
ISBN – 13: 9780340910085

Printed and bound in Great Britain by
Bookmarque Ltd, Croydon, Surrey

The paper and board used in this paperback are natural
recyclable products made from wood grown in sustainable
forests. The manufacturing processes conform to the envi-
ronmental regulations of the country of origin.

Hodder & Stoughton
A Division of Hodder Headline Ltd
338 Euston Road
London NW1 3BH
www.madaboutbooks.com

$\mathcal{A}$

ADVICE

Advice, like plants from other people's gardens, should be accepted with caution.

The Royal Horticultural Society (www. rhs.org.uk) gives excellent free gardening advice to its members. NEIGHBOURS with good-looking gardens are another source of useful advice. I give gardening advice via *The Times*' website, but only once a week.

AL FRESCO

Outdoor living is heaven. It can be transformed into hell by plastic furniture, which is to gardens what the wasp is to the picnic. You can buy attractive furniture for the same cost as the inexcusably ugly white plastic furniture sold in many garage forecourts. Or move your indoor furniture outdoors whenever there's a need. This is an eighteenth-century tradition – although, back then, it was orchestrated by liveried footmen.

ALPINES

These have often been displayed on ROCKERIES but, for those of us with limited space, an alpine trough or a bench in the greenhouse is a good alternative. Many of these exquisite plants need specialist soil conditions that require dedicated pots. Turn this to your advantage and display them around your front door, preferably at eye level. Visitors will then have visual entertainment as they wait for you to answer the door.

AUGUST IS A WICKED MONTH

Abutilon suntense has rescued many August borders from oblivion. It's tough and hardy in most areas of the UK and its hibiscus-like flowers give a Caribbean feel to even the most jaundiced garden.

Autumn shrubs

For those who don't live in an arboretum with dazzling autumn colour, here are some alternatives: *Solanum* and *Ceratostigma*.

Finally, *Arbutus unedo* has strawberry-like fruits, which appear in October and November, at the same time as its pinkish, bell-shaped flowers. Give it shelter.

Award of Merit

This cheery little sign on a plant's label means that, on the whole, it's a winner. Buy an Award-of-Merit plant and you can't go far wrong.

$\mathcal{B}$

BAGS OF WISDOM

Some of the more worthy, peat-free composts leach out of drainage holes as soon as you start watering. Put a tea bag over the hole(s), place broken crocks or polystyrene over that and the leaching will stop without the compost becoming sodden. Yes, used tea bags are fine.

BALLERINA

A tiny cornucopia may seem like an oxymoron but a little horn of plenty is better than none. This rule applies to small gardens. Apples and other fruits grafted onto dwarf rooting stock give miniaturised versions of a cornucopia. Ballerina (a single stem) and stepover (a stem bent sideways) fruit trees do the same for tiny gardens. And stepovers give high-interest edging for paths or beds with blossom in spring and fruit in autumn.

BARBEQUES

Do not have to look like burnt out hospital trolleys. They can be simple structures of brick or stone. And, when not in use, the true purpose of the 'barbie' can be disguised by a display of planted containers.

BEDDING

Before you turn the page, read on: bedding has a place in tasteful twenty-first-century schemes. For instance, the following combinations look great in large POTS: purple verbena massed with red geraniums; colourful, scented petunias; winter-flowering pansies; *Salvia patens* 'Cambridge Blue' surrounded by a ring of sedum. Talking of sedum, a pot of sedum looks good year round – it will need sharp drainage. And busy lizzies do the job in shady areas.

BIGGER IS BETTER

Big plants in a small garden make the area look bigger. This is counter-intuitive but it works. My first adult garden, a twelve-by-five metre inner-city plot, had giant lilies, giant hogweed, angelica and giant thistle. And a laburnum tree. The garden looked far larger than the clipped, low plantings of neat neighbouring plots.

BULBS

Plant a lot of them, especially if your version of gardening is slumping in the hammock with a glass of cool wine.

Bulbs will almost certainly flower. And you can increase the chance of that happening again and again by planting well and to the correct depth. Most bulbs like fertile, free-draining soil. Add a bit of horticultural grit to the soil or at least the base of the planting hole if your soil's heavy. Try to find the varieties that are used to being out in the garden (almost-black 'Queen of Night' tulips seem pretty bomb-proof), as opposed to more delicate specimens that prefer life in POTS. Then leave them alone. Squirrels, SLUGS and rot are the main enemies but, if the bulbs survive the first couple of years, they will probably survive for many more.

C

CANDY FLOSS

Cercidephyllum japonicum 'Heronswood Globe' grows to about twenty feet and is an ideal tree for medium-sized gardens. Few people know about it. In autumn its neat, rounded leaves turn dazzling orange and red, and send out a strong smell of candy floss. It likes a slightly acid soil and can manage dappled shade.

CARNATION, LILY, LILY, ROSE

Minimalist, maximalist, cottage, grand, public, stately or courtyard, a garden's not a garden without a lily and a rose.

Lilies abound in various horrid colours. Go for something simple and well-tried –

like the regal lily, which has big, white, scented trumpets tinted with maroon stripes. They are tough and relatively cheap.

Roses. Visit any rose garden where you can see the plants in the flesh before forking out for your own roses. Go for repeat-flowering varieties and, if you like them, don't be put off by the snobby glances directed towards tea roses.

As for carnations, those out-of-fashion members of the plant community, their peppery scent and Edwardian connections make them glamorous additions to the border.

CHEAP TOPIARY

Topiary looks great. Box topiary is expensive. Creating box topiary can take years

– which makes instant topiary appealing. Hawthorn grows fast, can be clipped into any shape, and looks great when it flowers. Choose a pink or red variety if you want a splash of colour. Alternatively, make a wire frame shape and grow ivy over it. Make the frame big otherwise the shape will vanish when the ivy takes hold. That's the problem with a lot of the commercial wire shapes: too small.

CHEATING

Only in some people's book... What's wrong with a few silk or plastic flowers when the border's looking empty?

The seventh-century Chinese Emperor Yangdi decked out his bare winter trees with silk flowers which means the system must be good enough for the rest of us.

And I know of at least one society

hostess who adds armfuls of cut flowers to her garden borders when guests are coming and the garden is below her high standards.

CHILDREN AND WATER

Can mix as long as you're careful. Many water features, from a single spout to a sculpture spraying water, look great and provide hours of interest provided the water lands on a bed of pebbles and filters down to an underground tank for circulation.

Or you can install a series of computer-controlled water jets timed to go off at random throughout the garden. This is a twenty-first-century version of the old water trick. Hours of squealing fun.

CHRISTMAS BOX

Also known as *Sarcococca*, this is an under-estimated little shrub. Its neat evergreen form provides good, low structure. Unlike regular box its tiny flowers produce a wonderful scent that pervades the garden in winter. I have seen it used, very successfully, as bed edging and hedging according to variety. *S. humilis* is good for edging and has flowers with a slightly pink tint. *S. hookeriana* can reach five feet tall.

CLIMBERS

(Or How to destroy a house)

Plants with aerial roots, like ivy and climbing hydrangeas, should be treated with extreme caution. They support themselves at the cost of WALLS, FENCES, houses and anything else that stands still long enough for them to sink their infernal little roots into. Give them a few years and they will demonstate that, in the long run, Mother Nature usually wins.

CELEBRATE YOUR COMPOST HEAP

Or bins. Or wormeries, come to that. These are the engine houses of the garden

– they create the luscious soil on which your plants will feed and thrive. Enjoy them. Sticking them behind the SHED, and hoping that nobody will notice them, rarely works. Use your imagination.

Add pretty finials to the tops of slatted wooden compost heaps. Make TRELLIS and bowers for wormeries. Paint pictures or *trompe l'oeil* on the sides of wormeries or compost surrounds. Or buy a beehive composter that does the job but looks indistinguishable from a hive. Search online and you'll find plenty.

COTTAGE GARDENS

Or gardens that have been, in Vita Sackville-West's words, 'ruffled about … into a wildly unsymmetrical mess and making it as near as possible into a cottage garden', are fine for those with time on their hands and tolerance for a bare-looking patch in winter. Informal garden style takes a lot more skill, time and patience than formal garden style.

D

DEAD HEADING

Such a simple process and one that will ensure a long flowering season for everything from geraniums to pansies to roses.

DEMOCRACY

Is not an easy gardening tool but, without it, your garden may not survive long if

you have a family/partner/lodgers/ inter-
fering friends. Discuss garden expecta-
tions with each of them. One person's
Eden may be another's Hades.

DESIGN

If you're busy or don't enjoy designing, get
someone to do it for you. The Society of
Garden Designers (www.sgd.org.uk) has a
list of tried-and-tested operatives. Look
carefully at their work. Meet the designer
and focus on whether or not they are
listening to you. Try to find a designer
who has his or her own construction team
or regularly works alongside one. That
may ensure a job finishes to the budget,
time and specification you want.

DIAMONDS

Catherine the Great, Empress of Russia, is said to have scattered them through her LAWN to make a pretty sparkly effect.

You could too, although they would play havoc with the mower blades. Better not perhaps. Instead the sparkle can come from a few discreet prisms tied to the branches of trees or larger shrubs to catch the light.

E

EDGES

A crisp lawn edge, like well-trimmed hair, always makes a good impression. Bed edges, curved or straight, look great when they are kept neat. At the beginning of the growing season, mark the edge of the bed with a plumb line or HOSE. Cut the edge with a spade. Dig out the area on the bed side of the edge to add definition to the edge and create a sort of mini-ha-ha. Yes, you can buy a motorised machine to do this, but is it really worth it? Maintain the new edge, with a long-handled edge trimmer, every time you mow. If your edges are defined by tiles, wooden planks or paving stones, keep the hard landscaping weed-free and maintain the mini-ha-ha on the bed side of the tiles, planks or pavors.

ENTRANCING ENTRANCES

An entrance sets the mood, style and ambiance of a place. Pay attention to it and visitors will pay attention to your garden.

The Chinese introduced moon gates, which frame the garden and, usually, make a visitor duck or bow as they enter. An entrance is a garden's headline – its definition – so a moon gate would be useless at the entrance to, say, an Italianate garden. Pillars, TRELLIS, sturdy gateposts, a farm gate, a flower-covered rustic arch, a steel arch, an arch of used garden TOOLS, concrete pillars, stone pillars, HEDGES, topiary peacocks and a fine Regency ironwork gate all make good entrances as long as the garden they lead into is appropriate.

EYECATCHERS

Are normally associated with rolling acres and the eighteenth century. Your garden may be on a different scale but it still deserves the odd eyecatcher. The odder the better, in fact. Eyecatchers are inter-

esting-looking objects designed to attract your attention towards an area that might otherwise be overlooked.

Eyecatchers can be anything from a painted fire hydrant to an ancient Roman statue, a decorated pot, a piece of sculpture, or a WATERING CAN. I've come across one successful sculpture/eyecatcher made from old headlights. This particular eyecatcher doubled as a light source for the drive.

F

FEBRUARY SHRUB

Camellias. When they were introduced to this country, these delicate-looking flowers used to be grown under glass. In fact they are tough enough to grow outside in most areas. They need a slightly acid soil but, hey, even in these soil-correct times, that can be arranged. For sheer variation *Camellia japonica* 'Lady Vanisittart' is good: it has five different colours, from red to white, all on one bush. The shape of 'Ave Maria' is perfect and *C. japonica* 'Tricolor' has the stripy look of *Rosa mundi*.

FENCES

Pretty ones need to be cherished. Treat them with one of the wood-preservative colours around. From *ver de gris* to red, there's no longer any excuse for using preservative brown. What's more, contemporary preservatives are water-based and therefore more environment-friendly.

Ugly fences, even if they are stable and strong, need to be smothered with CLIMBERS or removed. A HEDGE makes a good replacement or, if you have friendly NEIGHBOURS, maybe you could take out the boundary altogether.

FLAWLESS FLOORS

Just as a good setting transforms a diamond into jewellery, so a floor can transform a passable garden into a stunning plot. At best it will unite a design and encourage people into the garden. At worst it will make a gloomy and possibly dangerous place, if the slip-potential of the floor hasn't been dealt with.

Flooring choices are huge: intricate shell and pebble mosaic; bricks laid in various patterns; slate on its side or otherwise; different coloured bricks; gravel in all its various sizes and colours from white to red to blue to brown and yellow; raked gravel with a few well-chosen boulders; gravel mixed with patterns of bricks, timber or even spirals of steel or aluminium; decks (don't knock them –

they're fine in the right place); driftwood; nature's own paving such as York stone; terracotta tiles; frost-proof ceramic tiles; concrete squares (maybe in black and white like a chequers board); cobbles; glass; rubber; timber-edged squares each filled with a contrasting plant or material such as grass, gravel, brick, glass chippings and thyme.

FLOWER POTS

Terracotta pots are lovely but expensive. Plastic ones are cheap but ugly. Unless you paint them. Get each member of the family to paint a design, monogram or picture on some of the pots. Use acrylic paint. And, when the paint begins to flake, throw the pots away. Decaying plastic somehow lacks the allure of mossy terracotta.

FLYING HEDGES

Hornbeam and lime are the classic specimens for this treatment, but hawthorn, beech, judas and plenty more can be coaxed into airborne euphoria by stripping away the lower branches and joining the upper ones.

A flying hedge is handy for a small garden where you want privacy. Its trunk takes up little space but its top will shield your garden from prying eyes. It will also shield part of your garden from light – bear this in mind.

FOLIAGE

The fig leaf has been an enduring fashion statement since the Garden of Eden. Leafy gardens come in three forms:

The modern garden
Think hostas, fatsia, mahonia, deadnettles, artichoke, bay, conifers (within reason), cotinus, hebe, lemon balm, sage and, if you must, dreadful old heuchera.

The jungle approach
Increasingly appropriate planting in these globally warmed days. Go for: cordyline, bananas, gunnera, phormium, brugmansia, artichoke, melianthus, palms, actinidia, and tree ferns.

But bear in mind, your rainforest will have to be taken inside or fleeced up for winter.

Topiary
This gives low maintenance formality. Use box, bay, juniper, holly, hawthorn, ivy, beech, privet and firethorn.

FOUNTAINS

The simpler the better. The Tivoli fountains work because of their scale and Renaissance surroundings. Don't compete. A single jet looks great and is easy to install. And the sound is just as good as that made by all the revolting revolving, multi-coloured, multi-jets and water dimples available at garden centres.

FRONT GARDENS

A vexed subject and, tempting though it is to adopt a *laissez-faire* attitude resulting in a post-modern display of dustbins, cars and dead tricycles, there are more satisfying ways of dealing with the space.

Dead tricycles should be recycled. Dustbins should be given their own shelter, preferably with a green roof of anything from sedum to iris. Cars are never there all the time. If they are, get rid of them. The sliver of land between the wheels can be planted up with any low-growing plant from grass to thyme to ivy. POTS can improve areas of concrete. For further ideas see The Royal Horticultural Society's *Front Gardens* pamphlet which can be downloaded for free from www.rhs.org.uk/gardeningmatters.

G

GADGETS

Garden centres, like stationary shops, are dens of temptation. Treat their content with caution, particularly in the gizmos and gadgets section. 'Lawn-aerating spiked shoes' will cause you to stagger around the garden falling over regularly and doing more winding than aeration. Leaf blowers may look professional and manly but

they're noisy and only effective on dry leaves. Rakes are better and, for larger areas, a rotary mower will chop leaves as well as collecting them.

GARDEN ETIQUETTE

'You should have seen it last week,' or, 'It never looks good until next month,' are irritating traditional British chants. Break the mould. Like cooks who say that the fish is over/underdone or the salad dressing is a little strong/insipid, these phrases suck the pleasure out of the event. If your garden is not up to scratch, so what?

Let visitors enjoy what they will or ignore the whole thing.

GARDENERS

You may grumble about drought/sodden knees/weeds/disease/pests/expense but, if you are a Real Gardener, deep down you will be as happy as a lark.

But… you may not have time to do it all yourself, in which case you may have to hire a gardener. Throughout history they have been a mixed blessing. Get the right one and you are on the way to heaven. Get the wrong one and you've reached the serpent moment in the Garden of Eden.

GREEN GARDENING

So few garden chemicals are now available to the amateur gardener that you might as well learn how to garden along 'organic' lines. If you resort to using a chemical occasionally it's not the end of the world. The main thing is to persuade Nature to work alongside you – from frogs and birds to worms and lacewings. Gradually some kind of balance will build up and keep your garden from being overwhelmed by pest or disease. It won't eradicate either.

Everything you need to know about green gardening can be discovered via the charity, Garden Organic (www.hdra.org.uk).

A GREEN ROOF

One of these will extend your garden *and* help to save the world. The roof could be on your SHED, or even house – although it's always wise to check with the local planning authority first. Some Scandinavian countries grass their roofs and give sheep and cattle access. This cuts maintenance costs but involves shepherd/shepherdessing work which may or may not be your thing.

H

HAPPY PLANTS

Soil, like aspect, wind, frost, sun and rain, profoundly effects whether or not a plant will be happy. Get that right and you will save yourself time, money and heartache.

This isn't about Latin names or being the world's greatest botanist. This is common sense. Think about the provenance of a plant (look it up on the web) and think about what will make it feel at home.

If you'd always lived in a New York apartment and then you had to go and live on a Patagonian ice berg, how long would you last? And even if you did last, how would you look? Blooming with health and happiness?

HEDGES

Some can now be controlled by law, in theory. This is to protect people whose lives are thrown into Stygian gloom by leylandii or other evergreen hedges in neighbouring gardens. It's worth checking the law whether you are thinking about installing your own hedge or suffering the light deprivation from a neighbouring hedge. This link is helpful:

> http://news.bbc.co.uk/1/hi/uk_
> politics/4596685.stm

HEIGHT

Height can be achieved using CLIMBERS. It can also come from lollypop trees, interesting finials on top of TRELLIS or fencing, or an attractive weather vane on top of the house or SHED. My favourite vane is a flying pig. Alternatives include bats, shrimps, vintage cars, angels, George and dragons, a foot – I could go on. All can be found on the Internet.

HERBACEOUS BORDER

The jewel in the English country garden's crown and the duelling ground of upper-middle-class and upper-crust ladies for much of the twentieth century.

Strictly speaking, this is a border made up of perennials alone. Perennials make a great display until the frosts (and throughout winter for those who enjoy the sight of frosted seed heads). Without frost a herbaceous border looks rough in winter – soggy heaps of dead plants and lots of bare earth. That's fine if the border isn't going to be seen much from December to

April. If it can be seen from the house it may need a strong structure of evergreen or grey shrubs like box, choisya, lavender, teucrium (in mild areas), hebe and bay.

HONEYSUCKLE IS
THE SCENT OF SUMMER

Hedgerow or late Dutch is as common as muck and, like parsnips, underrated. Of course there are lots more CLIMBERS that will waft scent around your plot. But the rich honey scent of Cornish summers should be part of every garden. In milder areas flushes of the flowers can go on till Christmas. Aphids are sometimes a problem but honeysuckles are usually well behaved and trouble free. Hack them back in winter to keep them in order. Go for a form of common honeysuckle, *Lonicera periclymenum* 'Serotina' or 'Belgica'.

HOSES

Should be hidden completely in the form of black leaky pipes arranged around your beds – i.e. an automatic watering system.

Or they should make a feature by being coiled into wall-mounted boxes which can then be painted, *trompe l'oeil* style, with pictures of a blackbird on her eggs.

HOUSE AND GARDEN

Your garden and house have a relationship. To deny this fact is like trying to take a bone from a dog. Instead you should celebrate the relationship.

If your house is made from new brick, a weathered York-stone terrace is going to look odd. New brick or decking might be better materials. Or something unusual and adventurous like rubber or reinforced, slip-proof glass bricks (fantastic if you have a room under a terrace). Equally, if your house is old Cotswold stone, a reconstituted stone pavor terrace will look pretty awful – unless you find a company like these two, www.marshalls.co.uk and www.bradstone. com, among others, that make convincing faux stone as well as convincing types.

𝓘

IMITATION

Is the sincerest form of flattery. The National Gardens Scheme's *Yellow Book* is the best garden annual around. It lists thousands of gardens open for charity. The Red Cross runs a similar scheme. The *Good Gardens Guide* uses a starring system. Finally, the National Trust and English Heritage run some of the UK's most influential gardens from Sissinghurst in Kent to Wrest Park in Bedfordshire to Biddulph Grange in Staffordshire. You may have seen them on TV, you may have read about them but, like the difference between seeing an apple and tasting it, a visit will always reveal new delights and insights.

$\mathcal{K}$

KEEP YOUR HEADS UP

Staking is an undervalued art form. It's all down to timing and materials. Stake too early and your border is a sea of wire grids, bamboos and twigs. Too late and the plants are often unbiddable. Use hazel twigs for plants, like sweet peas, that need to twine. Even then their tiny tendrils sometimes need to be pointed in the right direction during the growing season.

Use green-stained canes or bamboos with garden twine or raffia to tie in plants like sunflowers or delphiniums. Some of the larger daisies and other clumps of flowers are best kept in order with one of the off-the-shelf staking systems made from green-coated wire. These can be pieced together to fit the size of the clump. For huge clumps of certain varieties of, say, rudbeckia, the best solution is to use tree- stakes and rope.

Learn one form of bow or knot and use it neatly and consistently throughout the garden.

KNOW YOUR BOUNDARIES

But don't be restrained by them. It could be that, by cutting a hole through a HEDGE or FENCE, you can make a window through to a pretty view. Make sure the HEDGE or FENCE is yours before you start work.

L

LAWNS

Lovely if you have the space and the right conditions. Do not attempt lawns under trees or any other shady area. They won't work. Ever. Put down a terrace or decking or Astroturf instead. Plastic grass comes in various grades and colours, just like the real thing. One of the companies that can be persuaded to supply small amounts, for front gardens or areas under trees for instance, is www.artificiallawn.co.uk

Established lawn has to be mown regularly. Adjust the blades so they are higher in periods of drought. Give the lawn a good raking out, aeration and feed every autumn to keep it emerald green instead of brown and weedy.

Finally, living alternatives to grass lawns don't work, by and large, unless you are prepared to accept bald or weedy bits in between your clumps of, say, thyme or camomile. Have a look at the so-called camomile lawn at Buckingham Palace. I rest my case.

LET THERE BE LIGHT...

Even at night. This is controversial, particularly among the star-gazing community. However lighting does not have to be kept on all the time. Nor should it be.

How many of us get to see our gardens during weekdays? The night's the time most of us get a chance to play outside.

How much better if the place is lit? Good lighting also makes the garden all the easier to use as an *al fresco* dining room.

Lots of options and they don't have to be expensive. Candle stubs/night lights in old jam jars are good. So are outdoor fairy lights and solar-powered lights that soak up energy in the day and give it out at night. Fibre optics can trace PATH edges, glide up tree trunks or provide flexible FOUNTAINS of light for children to play with.

LINES

Washing lines can be works of art if you are prepared to hang out your washing with an eye to colour and shape coordination. Even if this pastime doesn't appeal you should still hang your washing in the garden. It's cheaper and less damaging to your clothes, and to the environment, than using an electric clothes dryer.

So, you have a choice: line or whirligig? Retractable lines are a neat solution, if you have the space. If not, and the whirligig is the alternative, you need to think carefully about how you'll use it. They tend to dominate small gardens. Right now you and your partner are convinced you will collapse and store the whirligig whenever it's not in use. Who are you kidding?

M

MARY MARY

Came up with that great design feature –
cockle shells. I like using them along the
edge of beds or around a pot of BULBS or
perennials when the latter aren't doing
their stuff.

MAY TREE

May, *Crataegus*, or common hawthorn is a
versatile, attractive, cheap, fast-growing
plant that will make topiary, a HEDGE
(excellent for wild life) or a specimen tree.
All the *Crataegus* family show the same ver-
satility and includes specimens with
flowers ranging from red to pink to white.
What more can you ask of a plant?

N

NEIGHBOURS

The loveliest garden can be ruined by unfriendly/noisy/smelly/naked neighbours. Try to create a community atmosphere in your neighbourhood to prevent any unpleasantness. And if your neighbour (or their garden) is annoying you, try to sort out the problem as diplomatically and charmingly as possible.

NEW WAVE PLANTING

Noel Kingsbury is one of the aficionados of this style, which involves massed waves of perennials and grasses. This needs space. I would not attempt it in anything less than half an acre. But I am probably wrong. *Planting Design: Gardens in Time and Space* by Piet Oudolf and Noel Kingsbury explains the style in detail and gives you the chance to make up your own mind.

NON-NATIVE PLANTS

Relax. If you garden with native plants alone you'd be left with a handful of trees and not many more flowers. Who knows what grew here before the last ice age? And if God hadn't intended us to grow all these exotics he would never have given us such a forgiving climate. Without them we wouldn't have the horse chestnut, let alone the so-called English rose.

O

OIL TANKS

TRELLIS and CLIMBERS will do a traditional screening job on the tank, but how
about looking at it a different way? A tank
provides a smooth surface. Paint it white
and this could be your garden screen for
light images or films. If you'd prefer to

'lose' the tank, try a large mirror. It will have to be made from reinforced glass and all kinds of high specification stuff and will have to have its own sturdy frame independent of the tank – but it could look great, especially if you surround it with CLIMBERS to give the impression of a wide arch leading into another chunk of garden. A PATH up to the base of the mirror will complete the effect.

OPENING YOUR GARDEN

For the *Yellow Book* or for The Red Cross is the garden equivalent of scaling Everest. It will take years of painful preparation. When the last visitor trails away with a contented smile and a few yoghurt pots full of plants you raised, the sense of achievement is unbeatable.

All the same, the day can be challenging. Even if every blade of emerald grass is mown to uniform length and every flower is dripping with perfection, a few green-eyed garden monsters will find fault. Ignore them. They would have been picky about Eden too.

P

PATHS

Do more than guide your feet and protect LAWNS and beds: they direct your eye and add or detract from the pleasure of a garden. Therefore it's worth investing in them.

So many materials can be used to make a path: brick in every conceivable pattern; concrete (ditto); wood; rubber; crushed glass; pebbles; gravel; clinker; crushed shells.

If using particles – like gravel or glass – your foundations need to include geotextile or some other kind of weed-suppressing membrane. Otherwise you'll spend the rest of your life prising weeds out of the path and watching the path vanish miraculously into the lawn.

PICTURES

Keep taking them. There are two ways to take garden pictures:

* Close-ups of flowers and leaves (in the morning with a sprinkling of dew). These will convince you that you have a Chelsea-standard garden.

* Truthful pictures, taken from one end/side/above the garden. These can be kept in a locked drawer and taken out every now and then to remind yourself of all the bits that need your attention. Take pictures throughout the year to get an idea of what needs to be added when.

PLANTERS

Why confine yourself to expensive and, very often, dull pots, vases and urns from garden centres? Planters can be made from just about any container that has been pierced with drainage holes. Here

are a few ideas: aluminium buckets; WATERING CANS; chamber pots; horse troughs; olive oil cans whose gaily painted labels give a Mediterranean feel to a garden; painted dustbins; boats; trugs; wicker baskets lined with geotextile; milk churns; computer casing; cooking pots.

POTAGER

Is the posh name for a vegetable garden except that, in the words of the late great doyenne of such things, Rosemary Verey, if you want a potager, you will have to grow vegetables for eating elsewhere.

The point about a potager is that it is so well planned, as a visual rather than oral feast, that the removal of a row of carrots or a couple of lettuces will destroy the loveliness of the whole thing.

POTS OF GOOD LOOKS

Flower pots should be grouped together to make a pleasing whole. Think of the ascending ranks of basil and the lily-filled pots that line front steps of houses in provincial Italian towns. If you don't have steps, use pots of different heights to make a good arrangement and, when planning the planting, keep to some kind of theme to give unity to the group. It could be a recurring colour or a piece of topiary in every other pot, for instance.

PRAIRIE PLANTING

Think acres of flowers and grasses stretching into the distance and you have some idea of the ideal here – which makes it, like New Wave planting, an odd choice of style for the old English garden.

The idea is to let plants establish and self perpetuate, rather along the lines that William Robinson suggested in *The Wild Garden* over a century ago. The Garden House at Buckland Monachorum has an established and beautiful prairie planting whose voluptuous informality gives little idea of the work involved in establishing and maintaining the scene. Some local authorities have adopted a version of the style in which grasses dominate. These are big spaces. Try the style in a small backyard at your peril.

R

RARE PLANTS

Like forgotten symphonies and poems,
these plants are often rare/forgotten for a
good reason: they're rubbish.

Remember this when feeling over com-
petitive. You know the feeling which goes
something like this: 'I'll show the bastard

down the road what kind of gardener I am. I'm going to grow the impossible *Impossibilius uglii*. From seed. And carry off a Vietch medal from the Royal Horticultural Society to show just how good I am.'

Forget it. Stick to easy plants.

REFLECTIONS

A still pool of water reflects nearby plants and features and brings the sky – and light – into a garden. It will also bring a host of handy wildlife, from newts to birds to frogs and toads. All of which will help keep pests down to a minimum.

A still pool will almost certainly get bunged up with algae after a few years, particularly if you add fish (and even if you don't add them they tend to arrive anyway. No, I know fish don't have legs, but fish eggs arrive with herons and frogs). Barley straw will help (bung a weighted bag of the stuff into the pool) and so will a FOUNTAIN that can be turned on while you are away from the garden, if you feel strongly about keeping your pool calm and reflective.

RELAX

Gardens are about pleasure. If all it's giving you is grief, get rid of it. Move to an apartment.

If it's giving you grief because you're worried about what other people think about your garden, take courage. You may think your garden is badly maintained; your LAWN is a mix of bald and brown; you're incapable of remembering any common, let alone botanical plant names; your colour-coordinated border looks like the aftermath of a dolly-mixture explosion;

and your lighting scheme looks like a scene from a Gestapo movie. But, believe me, it will look better to an outsider.

So get out there and enjoy yourself.

S

SCENT

Evokes strong memories. Plant lots of smellies: jasmine, roses, lavender, rosemary, *Choisya*, *Philadelphus*, Daphne, thyme, winter and summer honeysuckle, lemon balm, viburnum, witch hazel, stocks, lilies, petunia, *Nicotiana sylvestris* and anything else that pleases your nose.

SCENTED SUMMER SHRUBS

June and July luxuriate in scented SHRUBS: pineapple broom or *Cytisus battandieri*, which needs a warm spot for its silvery leaves and yellow, pineapple-like flower heads to look their best; mock orange or *Philadelphus*, which puts up with almost any soil, likes sun and needs to have about a third of its flowering stems cut back after they've done their stuff. And roses. By July butterflies are floating around *Buddleia alternifolia*. They love this elegant, bomb-proof shrub, which will put up with the meanest soil so long as the drainage is good and the site sunny. Its weeping branches are covered with scented purple flowers through midsummer.

SCULPTURE

Don't include it unless you have a good eye, you've placed it with the help of the artists and you are *absolutely certain* that it will enhance your garden. Sculpture that is lovely in its own right won't necessarily look good in your garden. A garden that is lovely in its own right isn't necessarily the right place for a piece of sculpture.

SEATS

Gardeners rarely sit down. So they forget to install seats. Seats attract people into a garden and persuade them to focus on a particular view. And a well-chosen seat adds to the garden's beauty.

All kinds of benches can be bought from garden centres. Hanging seats and hammocks make romantic resting places. Tree trunks, with a sitting bit carved out, are great too. So long as the sitting bit has a drainage hole.

SEVEN HANDY CONTACTS

Garden Organic, for green gardening.
Ryton Organic Gardens, Coventry, Warwickshire CV8 3LG;
Tel: 024 7630 3517;
www.gardenorganic.org.uk

The National Council for the Preservation of Plants and Gardens (NCCPG)

The Stable Courtyard, Wisley Garden, Wisley, Woking, Surrey GU23 6QP; Tel: 01483 211465; www.nccpg.com

The National Gardens Scheme

NGS Hatchlands Park, East Clandon, Guildford, Surrey GU4 7RT; Tel: 01483 211535; www.ngs.org.uk

The Royal Horticultural Society

80 Vincent Square, London, SW1P 2PE; Tel: 020 7834 4333; www.rhs.org.uk

National Trust

PO Box 39, Warrington, WA5 7WD; Tel: 0870 458 4000; www.nationaltrust.org.uk

English Heritage
Customer Services Department,
PO Box 569, Swindon, SN2 2YP;
Tel: 0870 333 1181;
www.english-heritage.org.uk

The Garden History Society
70 Cowcross Street, London, EC1M 6EJ;
Tel: 020 7608 2409;
www.gardenhistorysociety.org

SHADE

Shady corners are shunned by some garden owners, who ignore them in the hope they'll go away. How much better to lavish attention and gorgeous plants on these areas. There are so many to choose from: sweetly scented *Sarcococca*; *Chaenomeles*, which flowers red, pink or white; ivy in all its forms; certain hydrangeas; periwinkle; ferns; foxgloves; hosta; busy lizzies. It's also worth trying Japanese anemones, peonies, giant lilies and Solomon's seal.

SHEDS

Can be beautiful. And they can be eyesores. Do not let your partner saunter off to the local shed shop unaccompanied. Go together and choose a shed that can house all your TOOLS as well as the contents of their den. And – unless you are lucky enough to come across a pretty, off-the-peg shed – buy a plain one with decent windows so that you can add turrets, flying buttresses, balconies, window boxes and whatever else takes your fancy. And cheer it up with a coat of wood preservative (now available in many colours). Also, it's amazing what a couple of roof finials or a weather vane can do.

SLUGS

Are a bad thing unless you like lace effect
on leaves or the amazing vanishing effect
of slugs on priceless BULBS.

Rich or squeamish gardeners should see
them off by applying a slug-predator
nematode.

Other gardeners can tramp about at night
after rain picking off slugs and throwing
them into buckets of water/dishes of salt.
Or stamping on them.

A plank of wood across a slug-infested area, or some scooped-out grapefruit halves will attract a crop of slugs by morning. Then you can decide on the method of dispatch.

SOUND

Adds or detracts to the pleasure of a garden. The sound of a FOUNTAIN will help block out neighbouring noises and add a restful note to the garden. The rustle of tree leaves and birdsong adds to the pleasure of the place. If nature doesn't provide enough of her own music why not add a garden sound system (these can be bought online – do not simply put your speakers outside) to add a little birdsong or wind-through-the-leaves sound? And music for parties. Check with the NEIGH-BOURS first and make sure you never allow your sounds to get annoying.

SPRING SHRUBS

In March, Japanese quince or, as it is more properly called, *Chaenomeles*, is strutting its stuff in red, orange, pink or white. It's a brilliant, go-anywhere shrub that will lean happily against a wall or make a HEDGE.

The subtle blue flowers of rosemary speckle April and May and its aromatic leaves are lovely all year round.

STEP OUTSIDE

Slopes are fine in large gardens and landscapes, but in small ones changes of level are best formalised. In other words, slopes should be transformed into terraces. This is not such a big deal so long as you can get some kind of digger on site. Failing that, a man with a spade.

The result will give your garden an extra dimension. A change of level can be used to define a different area – a dining spot from the children's play area for instance. And a short flight of steps between levels will draw visitors into the garden.

STEPPING STONES

In the form of anything from concrete pads to tree stumps, will direct visitors and protect LAWN/planting (they work well through borders). The advantage of stepping stones is that they are less intrusive than paths. When installing stepping stones through the lawn, remember to sink them low enough that the mower blades won't get mangled on the hard edges. The mower should be able to sail over the stepping stones without hesitation, repetition or deviation.

SUMMER HOUSES

I'm thinking more DIY-store than the palaces installed by royalty to get away from the hurly burly of state banquets and gong giving.

The great thing about modest summer houses is that they extend the season of your garden.

SURPRISES

Grand garden-design books will tell you that surprises are a Good Thing. I don't think I've ever been genuinely surprised in a garden unless you count the time I saw a flasher while working as the lowest form of gardener in Waterlow Park, London, just up the road from Karl Marx's grave. Human surprises aside, try to create contrasting atmospheres within a garden and to introduce more than can be seen at first

glance. Even a minute garden can sometimes conceal a tiny water feature until the
last moment.

SWINGS

Do not have to be plastic, brightly
coloured or designed for children or for
one person alone. Hung from a tree and
made from rope and timber, they look
attractive and form a good place for
romantics unaffected by motion sickness.

T

THEMES

Themes can unite a garden and add an intellectual dimension. A theme can be anything: a colour or a shape (like a circle or spiral); symbolic features representing ideas from science, maths or literature; or a narrative – like the Eden story. Try to find a theme that can incorporate most elements of your garden from the plants to the hard landscaping and TOOLS.

The Eden story has its pluses. An apple tree, fig and a tree of heaven can be planted. The HOSE can stand in as the serpent. The downside is that you will have to do the gardening while dressed in a fig leaf.

TOOLS

Are beautiful. This is in the modern tradition that good design always looks good. Well-loved and used tools develop a patina which adds to their attraction. Why hide them away? Hooks and nails driven into an inside wall beside the back door can make a stunning tool display area. The display should inspire rigorous cleaning of tools.

TREE HOUSES

Are far more alluring in principal than practice. Ask any parent who has erected a gorgeous tree house how much it has been used. The usual answer is: not a lot. On the other hand if a child is allowed to strap together a really dangerous structure in the arms of his or her favourite tree it will become a happy den for years.

Lavish and expensive tree houses as sold on the web are aimed at grown ups. In this country, tree houses have either to be elaborate, plumbed, glazed and heated

structures with some proximity to a tree, or a chilly room where visitors are occasionally forced to suffer while the tree-mad host realises arboreal childhood dreams.

Just remember that, on top of the expense, a tree house usually requires planning permission – and tolerant NEIGHBOURS if the structure overlooks their plot.

TRELLIS

Get it custom-made rather than buying the flimsy stuff from builders' merchants or garden centres. Use stout timber, and paint it with a water-based wood preservative.

Trellis is a great way to form boundaries that don't soak up all the light. And CLIMBERS have a lovely time scrambling up it.

W

WALLS

Attractive brick or stone walls need to be celebrated. Don't smother them in CLIMBERS. Use a single climbing rose or a meek clematis (there aren't many) to enhance the colour or texture of the wall.

Breeze-block walls deserve to be smothered and, so long as they are well built, they can be hidden by ivy. This will attract plenty of nesting birds. It will also attract a host of snails. Don't plant snail food like BULBS, crambe, sunflowers and hosta near the wall.

WATER TRICKS

From fifteenth-century Italy to eighteenth-century Britain, water tricks were part of many grand gardens. The usual form was a sudden and unexpected jet of water from a hidden source on a terrace. Visitors would be lured to a given spot by, say, a stunning view. As the victim stood there, a water jet would squirt from below.

Today's equivalents are mist machines, which spread fog whatever the weather, or computer-controlled water jets concealed randomly through the gravel or decking in a garden.

WATERING CANS

Choose carefully. A well-balanced can (pick them up by their handles and compare the feel of them) makes watering more comfortable and, by and large, looks better than a badly-balanced can. An aluminium can looks great and makes a feature in its own right. Some plastic cans, particularly the deep green ones, can be attractive, too.

Painted watering cans make good design features, which means one less tool to clear away at the end of the day. If you can't think of what to paint, traditional canal barge pictures look good. Use enamel paint for metal, acrylic for plastic.

WEEDING

Even if you want and can afford a gardener, try to do some of the weeding yourself. There are three reasons:

* it will make you see your garden in a different light and make you acknowledge the areas where it's not as good as it could be;

* even well-intentioned professional gardeners are less likely than you to weed around dear little seedlings of peonies/nigella/angelica and every other garden plant that wants to replicate itself;

* if you try to clear your mind of everything bar seedlings and weeds, weeding can induce an almost trance-like state of karma.

WILDFLOWER PLANTINGS

Are alluring until you consider that gardens are unnatural, or, as the poet Andrew Marvell put it:

Luxurious man, to bring his vice in use,
Did after him the world seduce,
And from the fields the flowers and
    plants allure,
Where nature was most plain and pure
He first enclosed within the garden square
A dead and standing pool of air,
And a more luscious earth for them did
    knead.

If you're determined to have wildflowers a layer of 'luscious earth' will have to go.

Wildflower meadows and Postcode Plants (www.nhm.ac.uk/fff) will indicate which flowers to use.

WILDLIFE POOL

St Tropez-style pools attract some extremely wild life but only for a few months a year. So much more satisfying to have a pool, which gives year-round pleasure – from an icy sparkle in winter, to nature's playground for the rest of the year. Any pool, however small or formal, will attract wildlife.

The great thing about wildlife is that it helps build an ecosystem that will keep pest and disease at an acceptable level as well as

adding another dimension; from darting wagtails to the gentle croak of frogs.

WILLOW

Is the can-can girl of the garden world. Never mind that she inspired some of William Morris's iconic Arts and Crafts designs. She's colourful, cheap, fast growing, reliable and one of the easier plants to grow. Push a stick of willow into the ground and, by and large, it will root and thrive. Some willows can grow nearly three metres a year. The colour of young shoots ranges from lurid green to orange, red, violet and brown depending on variety.

WINTER BLUES

Gardeners approach winter in two ways: some pretend it isn't happening; others defy the gloom with colour.

If you can persuade yourself to be part of the second category, here are a few ideas:

Callicarpa bodinieri var. *giraldii* 'Profusion' or *C. dichotoma* is a cheery plant that produces shiny purple/mauve berries in winter.

The slender young stems of *Cornus alba* 'Sibirica' give a fiery splash of red in the dead of winter.

Good old WILLOW, pollarded right down to the ground, will send up shoots of purple, red, orange or yellow depending on the variety.

Golden Winter aconites, mauve *Cyclamen coum*, and wallflowers like 'Bowles Mauve' bloom in winter. Flowering cherries (*Prunus* 'Fudan-zakura' and *Prunus x subhirtella*) produce winter blossom. Some plants, like *Daphne bholua* var. *glacialis* 'Gurkha' and *Viburnum x bodnantense*, give scent as well as colour.

WORMS AND THEIR CASTS

Learn to love them. They help make plants strong and productive. If worm casts become a serious problem, sprinkle sulphur on the lawn to lower its acidity or you can find other ideas at www. oxford croquet.com. Alternatively, distribute the casts around the lawn and bask in the knowledge that worm casts have been cool since 2006 when they helped win a gold medal for Chris Beardshaw's Chelsea Flower Show garden.